D1568537

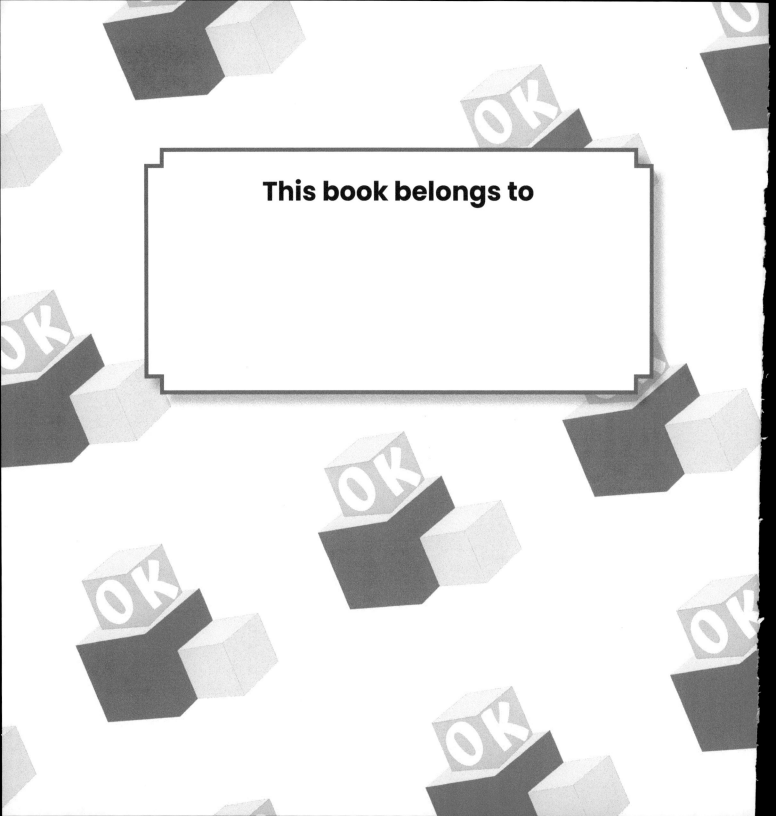

This book belongs to

Dedicated to Khalil

OH KHALIL

and the COLOR BLOCK BANDIT!

By Khadijah Fair
Illustrated by Book Ruffell

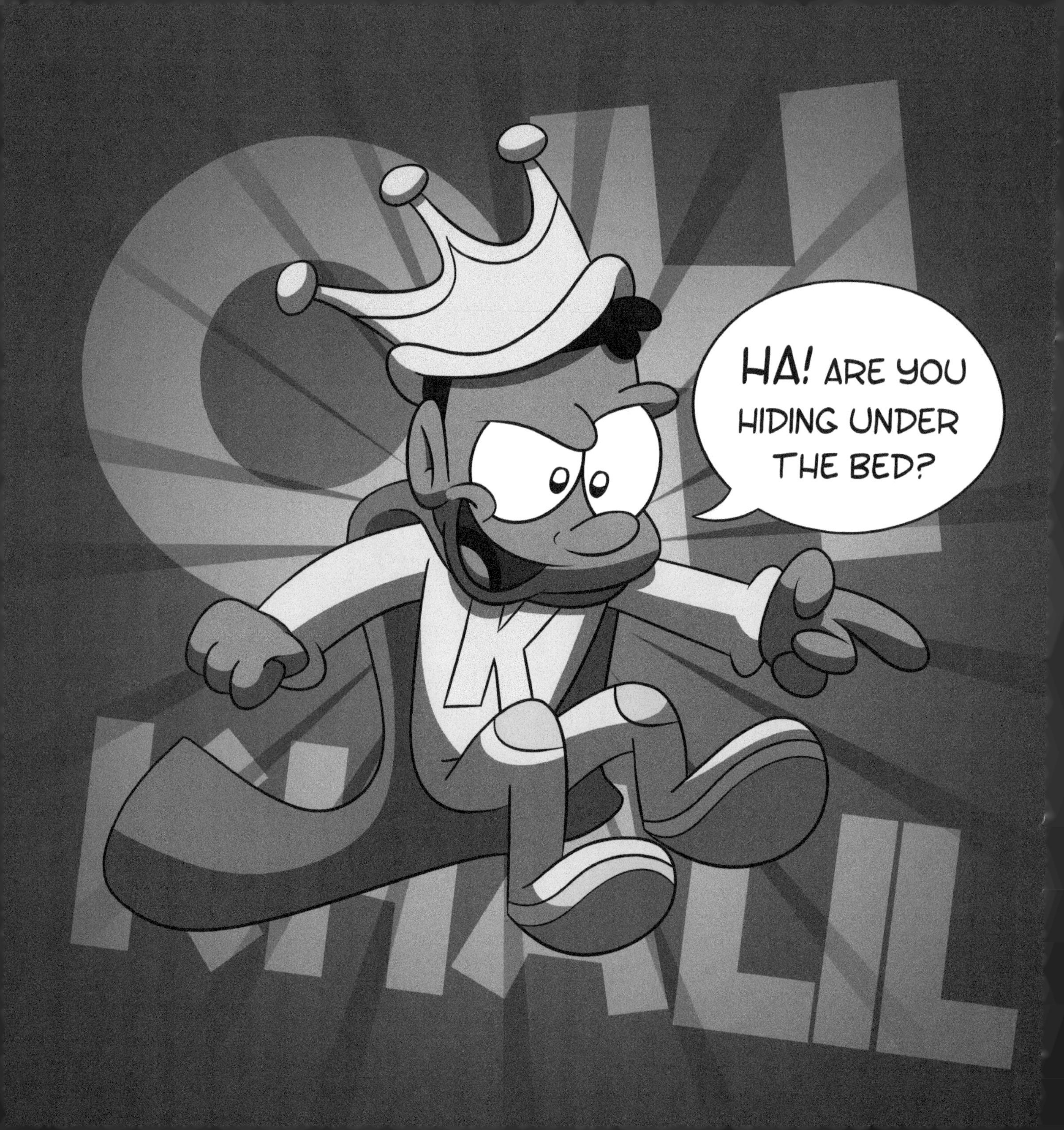
HA! ARE YOU HIDING UNDER THE BED?

Activity

What colors are Khalil's color blocks?

How many color blocks does
Khalil have?

How many crayons did you see in
Khalil's bedroom?

How many times did you see
Jellybean?

What time is shown on the
Living room clock?

Learn the Alphabet in **American Sign Language**

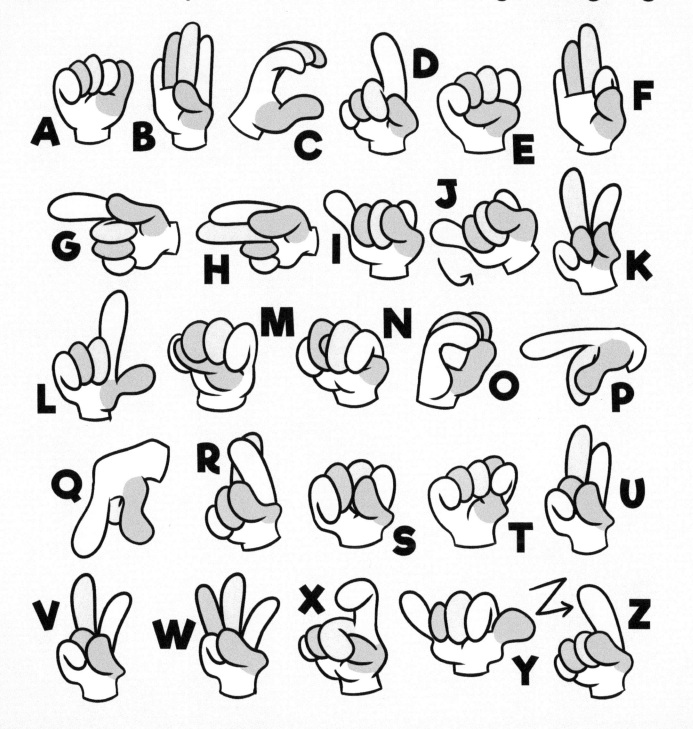